This

D0560444

THE REVEREND R.H. WHITTINGTON MBE

CHAPLAIN

THE ROYAL HOSPITAL CHELSEA
ROYAL HOSPITAL ROAD
LONDON   SW3 4SR

TEL WORK: 020 7881 5234
TEL HOME: 020 7881 5260
FAX: 020 7881 5490
EMAIL: chaplain@chelsea-pensioners.org.uk
MOBILE: 07979 360025

A catalogue record for this book is available from the British Library

Published by Ladybird Books Ltd
A Penguin Company
Penguin Books Ltd, 80 Strand, London WC2R 0RL, UK
Penguin Books Australia Ltd, Camberwell, Victoria, Australia
Penguin Group (NZ) Ltd, 67 Apollo Drive, Rosedale, North Shore 0632, New Zealand

10
© LADYBIRD BOOKS LTD MCMXCVIII. This edition MMVI

ISBN-13: 978-1-84422-945-1

Printed in China

Dick
Whittington

illustrated by Terry Gabbey

Once upon a time, there lived a boy called Dick Whittington. He had no parents, and he had no money.

One day Dick said, "I'm going to London to look for work."

London was a long way away.
Dick walked for miles and miles.
It took him a long time and when
he got there, it was not at all
like his home.

In London there were lots of big houses and lots of shops.

"There will be work for me here," said Dick.

So Dick went to all the big houses and all the shops, but there was no work for him.

Dick had nowhere to go. He was so tired that he went to sleep in the doorway of a big house. A cook came out of the door.

"You can't sleep here!" she said. "Go away at once."

11

Just then, the man who lived in the house came home. He was called Mr Fitzwarren, and he was very rich.

"This boy has nowhere to go," he said to the cook. "Let him work in the kitchen."

13

So Dick started work in the kitchen. He worked hard all day, and Mr Fitzwarren was very pleased.

At night, he slept in a room at the very top of the house. The room was only big enough for Dick's bed.

But every night, as Dick tried to sleep, rats and mice jumped about on his bed.

"A cat would catch all these rats and mice," said Dick. "I will go and buy a cat."

17

The next day, Dick saw a woman who had a beautiful cat to sell.

"Can this cat catch rats and mice?" said Dick.

"This cat is the best rat and mouse catcher in the whole of London," said the woman.

"Then I would like to buy her," said Dick.

Dick gave the woman one penny, and he took the cat home.

When Dick went to bed that night, the cat chased the rats and mice away. At last, Dick had a good night's sleep.

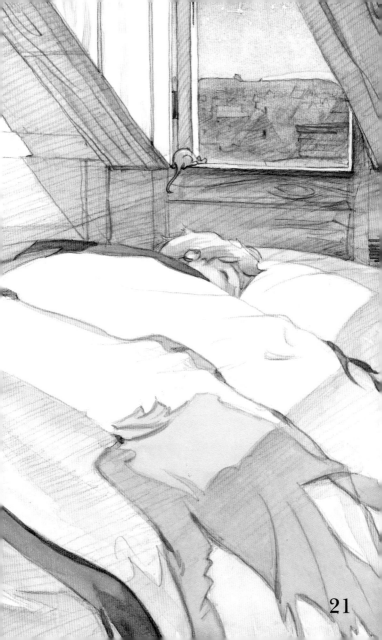

21

Mr Fitzwarren had a beautiful daughter called Alice. Alice wanted to help Dick.

"My father has lots of ships," she said. "He sells goods to rich people in countries far away. Give him something to sell, and then you can be rich."

23

"What can I sell?" said Dick. "All I have is my cat."

"Then my father will take your cat and sell it," said Alice.

Dick didn't want to sell his cat, but he wanted to please Alice.

Dick gave his cat to Mr Fitzwarren.

"This cat is the best rat and mouse catcher in the whole of London," said Dick. "Will you sell her for me?"

"Yes," said Mr Fitzwarren.

Dick missed his cat. Every night, the rats and mice came back and jumped about on Dick's bed. This made Dick very unhappy.

"I don't like London," said Dick. "I'm going back home."

So the next day, Dick set out for home. Just as he was leaving London, he heard the church bells.

"Turn again, Whittington,
  Lord mayor of London.
  Turn again, Whittington,
  Thrice mayor of London."

"The bells are calling me back to London!" said Dick.

So Dick didn't leave London, he turned and went back to Mr Fitzwarren's house. When he reached the house everyone was asleep. No one had seen him leave.

As Dick was sleeping in his bed, Mr Fitzwarren's ship was sailing to a country far away. The King and Queen of the country wanted to buy some goods. As he was leaving the ship to go and see them, Mr Fitzwarren took Dick's cat with him.

The King and Queen had a beautiful palace, but there were mice and rats running all over it.

Mr Fitzwarren said, "I have a cat that can help you."

And Dick's cat chased all the rats and mice away.

37

The King and Queen wanted to buy Dick's cat, but the cat wanted to go home.

The King and Queen said, "This beautiful cat has helped us. Take her home, and give this money to her master."

So Mr Fitzwarren took the cat back to London.

When Mr Fitzwarren came home, he gave the money and the cat to Dick. Dick was pleased to have the money, and he was even more pleased to see his cat again. The money made him rich, and not long after, he married Alice.

So Dick, Alice and the cat lived happily ever after.

And the people of London made Dick the lord mayor – just as the bells had said.

Read It Yourself is a series of graded readers designed to give young children a confident and successful start to reading.

Level 4 is suitable for children who are ready to read longer stories with a wider vocabulary. The stories are told in a simple way and with a richness of language which makes reading a rewarding experience. Repetition of new vocabulary reinforces the words the child is learning and exciting illustrations bring the action to life.

About this book

At this stage children may prefer to read the story aloud to an adult without first discussing the pictures. Although children are now progressing towards silent, independent reading, they need to know that adult help and encouragement is readily available. When children meet a word they do not know, these words can be worked out by looking at the beginning letter (*what sound does this letter make?*) and other sounds the child recognises within the word. The child can then decide which word makes sense.

Nearly independent readers need lots of praise and encouragement.